Radical Renovation

JAMES A. HARNISH

Radical Renovation

Living the Cross-Shaped Life

A LENTEN STUDY FOR ADULTS

ABINGDON PRESS / Nashville

RADICAL RENOVATION: LIVING THE CROSS-SHAPED LIFE
A LENTEN STUDY FOR ADULTS

Copyright © 2008 by Abingdon Press

This book is printed on acid-free paper.

Library of Congress Cataloging-in-Publication Data

Harnish, James A.
  Radical renovation : living the cross-shaped life : a Lenten study for adults / James A. Harnish.
    p. cm.
  ISBN 978-0-687-64548-0 (pbk. : alk. paper)
  1. Bible. N.T. Mark--Devotional literature. 2. Lent--Meditations. I. Title.

  BS2585.54.H37 2008
  242'.34--dc22

                    2007031364

08 09 10 11 12 13 14 15 16 17 — 10 9 8 7 6 5 4 3 2 1

MANUFACTURED IN THE UNITED STATES OF AMERICA

In memory of Glenn Jackson,
for whose life, faith, and friendship,
I sing a broken hallelujah

Contents

Introduction

Ty Pennington, the hunky, hyperenergetic host of the television show *Extreme Makeover: Home Edition*, was in our neighborhood recently. He brought his construction crews and television cameras to Tampa's Davis Islands to build a new home for the Tate family just a few blocks away from our parsonage. The Tates lost everything they owned when a small, private airplane skidded off the runway at the Peter O. Knight Airport and exploded in flames in their living room.

The rebuilding of the Tate home followed the familiar pattern of the television show. First, the *Extreme Makeover* producers find a family who are in desperate need of a new home but utterly incapable of providing it. Then the designers go to work behind the scenes to prepare everything for the week of construction. In this case, it involved major cooperation with the city to resolve permit and design issues related to the risks of hurricane and flood damage. The actual work begins when Ty sends the family off for a week's vacation and calls in the bulldozers to tear down the old house. By the end of the week, the new Tate home was completed. The show always ends with laughter, tears, and shouts of joy as the family moves into their renovated home to live their lives in a whole new way.

Extreme Makeover: Home Edition provides a powerful metaphor for the kind of "radical renovation" that God intends to do in each of our lives. In the fourth century, Saint Augustine looked at the wreck he had made of his life and prayed,

> The house of my soul is too small for you to enter: make it more spacious by your coming. It lies in ruins: rebuild it. Some things are to be found there which will offend your gaze; I confess this to be so and know it well. But who will clean my house? To whom but yourself can I cry? (*The Confessions*; page 6)

9

As a Shakespeare fan, I still prefer the way the Elizabethan version of that prayer captures the urgency of it: "Narrow is the mansion of my soul; enlarge Thou it, that Thou mayest enter in. It is ruinous; repair Thou it!"

Talk about a radical renovation! God intends nothing less than the total reconstruction of our lives, so that we can become the kind of people in whom the living Christ can take up residence and through whom the Kingdom—the redemptive reign, loving purpose, and saving will of God revealed in Jesus Christ—can become a tangible reality in this world. The promise is that when God rebuilds the house of our lives, it will perfectly fulfill the design God intended for us from the beginning. St. Paul used construction imagery to describe God's intention for us when he said that in union with Christ, we are being "built together with all the others into a place where God lives through his Spirit" (Ephesians 2:22 GNT).

In a more specific way, "radical renovation" is also a powerful image of what can happen in our lives during the season of Lent. Just the way the great cathedrals were built in the shape of a cross, the traditional Lenten disciplines invite us to allow the Spirit of God to reshape the way we think, act, and live into the likeness of Jesus on his way to the cross. The apostle Paul gave the master design of a cross-shaped life in his letter to the Philippians:

> Think of yourselves the way Christ Jesus thought of himself. He had equal status with God but didn't think so much of himself that he had to cling to the advantages of that status no matter what. Not at all. When the time came, he set aside the privileges of deity and took on the status of a slave, became *human*! Having become human, he stayed human. It was an incredibly humbling process. He didn't claim special privileges. Instead, he lived a selfless, obedient life and then died a selfless, obedient death—and the worst kind of death at that—a crucifixion. (Philippians 2:5-8 *The Message*)

The apostle personalized the design of a cross-shaped life when he wrote autobiographically:

> I have been crucified with Christ; and it is no longer I who live, but it is Christ who lives in me. And the life I now live in the flesh I live by faith in the Son of God, who loved me and gave himself for me. (Galatians 2:19-20)

Jesus himself offered the call to a cross-shaped life when he said, "If any want to become my followers, let them deny themselves and take up their cross daily and follow me" (Luke 9:23).

When I was growing up in the pre-Vatican II days of the 1950s, we Protestants didn't pay much attention to Lent. Lent was something Catholics did. I remember Catholic kids at school talking about what they were "giving up" for Lent. It sounded like a good time to give up *broccoli*, to me! It was later that I came to understand the value of fasting as a form of sacrificial discipline through which our bodies experience a change that calls us into a deeper reflection on the sacrifice of Christ for us.

Instead of "giving up" something for Lent, I invite you to "take up" something for Lent this year. We can take up the cross by maintaining a daily discipline for scripture reading and prayer; by faithful participation in worship; by finding a place for Christian community in a small group; by tithing (or giving one-tenth of) our income for God's work through the church; and by giving ourselves in service to people in need, in the spirit of the One who came among us not to be served, but to serve (see Matthew 20:28).

The "Extreme Makeover" of the Tate home began in the dust and ashes of destruction. In the same way, our Lenten journey begins with ashes, the dust of our mortality, the sign of our need for the internal renovation of our lives, marked on our foreheads with a cross on Ash Wednesday. But the promise is that the radical renovation of our lives will end in the joy and laughter of Easter morning, and that it will be the beginning of a whole new way of life!

Questions for Discussion or Reflection

1. In your own words, describe the idea of a "Radical Renovation." What does it involve? *a very noticeable change*
2. Reread the prayer by Saint Augustine from his *Confessions*. What are your thoughts on this prayer? How do you identify with or relate to it? When have you felt or experienced what Augustine prayed? *I don't spend enough time with God so my need for him becomes small*
3. Reread Philippians 2:5-8 and Galatians 2:19-20. What does the term "cross-shaped life" convey to you in light of these passages of scripture? *make sacrifices, go outside your comfort level.*

4. What is your personal experience with Lent? Have you ever "given up" something for Lent? What spiritual disciplines will you "take up" this year?
5. What does Ash Wednesday mean to you?

Prayer

Lord, who throughout these forty days
for us didst fast and pray,
teach us with thee to mourn our sins
and close by thee to stay.

As thou with Satan didst contend,
and didst the victory win,
O give us strength in thee to fight,
in thee to conquer sin.

As thou didst hunger bear, and thirst,
so teach us, gracious Lord,
to die to self, and chiefly live
by thy most holy Word.

And through these days of penitence,
and through thy passiontide,
yea, evermore in life and death,
Jesus, with us abide.

Abide with us, that so, this life
of suffering over past,
an Easter of unending joy
we may attain at last.

("Lord, Who Throughout These Forty Days," Claudia F. Hernaman, 1873)

Discipleship: The Design of the Cross-Shaped Life

Scripture: Read Mark 8:27-38.

I n the fall of 2004, Jamie Dolan was the sole survivor of a random shooting at a Radio Shack store in St. Petersburg, Florida, in which two other employees and the gunman were killed. A bullet to his head left Jamie blind. A year later the Dolan family became the center of national attention when the *Extreme Makeover: Home Edition* crew came to St. Petersburg to build Jamie, his wife, and their three children a new home.

They bulldozed the Dolan's forty-four-year old house and rebuilt it to meet the needs of a blind man and his family. The show ended, as they all do, with a lump in every throat and a tear in every eye as the family moved in to begin their lives in a whole new way.

In a deeper sense, an extreme makeover, a "radical renovation," is precisely what God wants to do in and through us. The Bible says that God's work of salvation calls for a total reconstruction of our sin-distorted lives and of this sin-damaged world, so that the living Christ can take up residence in us and so that through us God's kingdom can become a tangible reality in this world. Salvation is nothing less than a radical renovation of cosmic proportions.

In 1995, we began a nonstop renovation project at Hyde Park United Methodist Church that continued for eight years. Across the time, we tore down, remodeled, or built new buildings on every square inch of three blocks in the city of Tampa, including the sanctuary, which was originally built in 1907. The renovations didn't always move along the way we planned. There were surprises along the way. But the project resulted in facilities in which the congregation could live, grow, and be in ministry for many years ahead.

There were times along the way when I felt like the frustrated homeowner described in Helen Kromer's 1960s satirical musical review, *For Heaven's Sake*. The homeowner invited God into his home to do what he thought would be some minor repair work. The homeowner knew that his home needed new gutters and a new coat of paint. He was aware of rotting floor boards and cracked plaster. He thought he could get God to do some modest patch and repair work.

To the homeowner's surprise, God came in and began a major rebuilding of the entire house! The homeowner fumed about the "divine house wrecker" who ripped out rotten beams, tore open picture windows in the walls of his cozy hideaway, added new floors, and launched a nonstop rebuilding project that began to turn what was a quiet little bungalow into a castle fit for a king. The homeowner began to feel as if the house no longer fit his old, small-house lifestyle and finally told God that it felt more like a place where God would live. That's when the divine renovator told the homeowner that the purpose of the renovation was for God to take up residence in him.

Make no mistake about it. When God begins a work of interior renovation in our small, narrow, self-addicted lives, God has a big idea. God's renovation plan is to rebuild our little lives into a place where God can take up residence and be at home.

A good starting point for understanding the design of the radical renovation God intends to do in our lives is the hinge passage upon which Mark's Gospel turns. It's the story of Peter's audacious affirmation that Jesus is the Christ; the Messiah; the finite, human expression of the essential character of the infinite, almighty God. (See Mark 8:29.) Suddenly, everything shifts in verse 31 when Mark records:

> Then [Jesus] began to teach them that the Son of Man must undergo great suffering, and be rejected by the elders, the chief priests, and the scribes, and be killed, and after three days rise again.

Suffering, rejection, and death were clearly not a part of the design that Peter had in mind. Mark uses a very strong verb to say that Peter

14

"rebuked" Jesus. It's the same verb Mark uses to describe the way Jesus rebuked evil spirits. Peter has just declared that Jesus was the Messiah, the one who comes to represent God's reign and rule in this world; but now, the first time Jesus says something that doesn't fit into Peter's plan, he rebukes Jesus, turns his back on him, and heads off in the opposite direction. It makes me wonder if there might not be a little bit of Peter in most of us.

Isn't there something in most of us that would like to have just enough of Christianity to be religious, but not so much that it disrupts the assumptions upon which we live?

Isn't there something in us that wants to add a safe, predictable dash of spirituality to our lives, but doesn't want to be confronted with anything that challenges the basic perspective of the culture around us?

Isn't there something in us that longs to know that God can save us, but is not so keen on having a God who actually expects us to become a part of his saving work in the world?

Aren't there times when we would like God to come in to do a little repair work, but we're not so sure we want him doing major renovation?

When Peter rebuked Jesus, he may not have been all that different than we are—just a little more honest and a lot gutsier in expressing it!

Mark does an interesting thing in telling the story. He turns Peter's words back on him by using the very same verb to say that Jesus "rebuked" Peter and told him, "Get behind me, Satan! For you are setting your mind not on divine things but on human things" (Mark 8:33).

Jesus says that there is a Continental Divide that runs through the center of our souls. It divides two ways of living, thinking, and being. One way is to set our minds on the ordinary, human design for thinking and living. It's not necessarily bad; it's just ordinary. It's the ordinary perspective of ordinary people living by the ordinary assumptions of the ordinary world. The opposite option is to set our minds on God's design. It is the extraordinary way of living that sees all of life from the perspective of the saving will and life-giving way of God that Jesus modeled by going to the cross.

Mark uses another strong verb when Jesus tells Peter, "You are *setting your mind* not on divine things but on human things" (8:33,

15

emphasis added). Luke uses the same expression to describe the way Jesus "*set his face* to go to Jerusalem" (Luke 9:51, emphasis added). Paul uses it when he tells the Colossian Christians, "*Set your minds* on things that are above" (Colossians 3:2, emphasis added). It describes a radical reorientation of our thinking that results in an equally radical reorientation of our living.

Do you remember Copernicus? He figured out that the sun, not the earth, is at the center of the solar system and that the earth revolves around the sun, not the other way around. Talk about a radical renovation! His discoveries totally reconstructed everything we thought we knew about the earth and its relationship to the rest of the solar system. It resulted in a total reorientation of the way we think and live on this planet.

Jesus calls us to nothing less than a Copernican revolution in the way we think and live. Contrary to most cultural assumptions, my little world is not the center of the universe. It's not all about me. The universe does not revolve around my self-interest. The most important question in life is not "What's in it for me?" The gospel is not a self-help manual to make life go a little better. Jesus calls us to a radical reorientation in the way we think that leads to an equally radical redirection of the way we live. Or, to return to our original metaphor, Jesus is nothing less than a divine version of Ty Pennington, who comes, not to do a little repair work, but to bring a total reconstruction of the way we think that results in an extreme makeover of the way we live.

Martin Luther, the sixteenth-century reformer, borrowed the Latin phrase "*homo incurvatus in se*" from Saint Augustine. It means "man curved in on himself." Luther wrote, "Our nature . . . is so deeply curved in on itself that it not only bends the best gifts of God towards itself and enjoys them . . . but it also fails to realize that it so wickedly, curvedly, and viciously seeks all things, even God, for its own sake" (*Lecture on Romans* [1515]. Quoted by David S. Yeago in "The Catholic Luther," *First Things* [1996]; http://www.firstthings.com/article.php3?id_article=3838).

The principle of *homo incurvatus in se* was captured in Greek mythology in the story of Narcissus. He was so good-looking that the god Nemesis cursed him to fall in love with his reflection. The more Narcissus looked at himself, the smaller he became until there was nothing left but a little white flower. Eugene Peterson wrote, "Narcissus got smaller and smaller and smaller until there was no

Narcissus left: he had starved to death on a diet of self" (*Christ Plays in Ten Thousand Places* [Grand Rapids: William B. Eerdmans, 2005], page 243).

Starving to death on a diet of self is an accurate diagnosis of the most malignant cancer in the human heart. The evidence is that *homo incurvatus in se* is deadly. Life turned in on itself gets smaller and smaller until there is nothing left that can be called life. But in a sin-distorted world, this is the ordinary, human design for living and thinking.

By contrast, Jesus called his followers to a way of thinking that turns the mind-set of the world inside out. He defined the fundamental irony of the cross-shaped life when he said, "Those who want to save their life will lose it, and those who lose their life for my sake, and for the sake of the gospel, will save it" (Mark 8:35).

It's true, you know. If you try to save your life, hold it, hoard it, protect it, squeeze it tightly to your chest, you will squeeze the life right out of it. A life centered in itself ultimately shrivels up and dies. But if you lose your life, if you release your life, if you throw yourself with almost reckless abandon into the way of life that Jesus taught, you will find it! You'll find real life, abundant life, resurrection life that can never be put to death.

Jesus is not looking for fans like the ones who line the red carpet in Hollywood for the Academy Awards. Jesus is not looking for objective observers who will stand off to the side and coldly critique what he has to say. Jesus is looking for disciples: ordinary men and women who will allow their lives to be transformed by the extraordinary self-giving love of God supremely revealed at the cross. Jesus is calling disciples who will allow the mind-set with which he lived, died, and rose again to become the mind-set in which they live, with which they die, and through which they are raised to new life. It's the basic design of a cross-shaped life, and that's exactly what God intends to build in each of us.

Questions for Discussion or Reflection

1. When you look at your own experience, have you ever felt like a homeowner who invited God in to do some repair work and then discovered that God had a major renovation in mind? How did you respond? What difference did it make?

17

2. Read Mark 8:27-33 aloud, with one member of the group reading the narration, one reading the words of Jesus, and another reading the words of Peter. How do you think Peter felt when he "rebuked" Jesus? How did Peter feel when Jesus "rebuked" him?
3. What does it mean for you to "set your mind" on something? How has this chapter helped enlighten the difference between setting your mind on human things and on divine things?
4. Where do you see evidence of *"homo incurvatus in se"*—life turned in upon itself—in our culture? How have you experienced it in your own life?
5. Reread Mark 8:35. What does it mean for you to live into the truth of this scripture? What action can you take to move in that direction?

Prayer

Almighty God, whose most dear Son went not up to joy but first he suffered pain, and entered not into glory before he was crucified; Mercifully grant that we, walking in the way of the cross, may find it none other than the way of life and peace; through Jesus Christ your Son our Lord. . . . Amen. (*Book of Common Prayer*, 1979, page 220)

Focus for the Week

Jesus' design for discipleship calls us to a radical reorientation of our lives.

Servanthood: A Peculiar Way to Greatness

Scripture: Read Mark 9:33-37, 10:32-45.

T he disciples just didn't get it. I wonder if *we* do.
Jesus had told them clearly that they were on their way to Jerusalem where he would face rejection, suffering, and death. They were on their way to the cross. But as they were making their way down the dusty roads of Palestine, Jesus was eavesdropping on the disciples' conversations. Over dinner that evening he asked the disciples, "What were you arguing about on the way?" (Mark 9:33).

Mark says the disciples were silent. It must have been an awkward silence, filled with a lot of shuffling of feet, twiddling of fingers, and staring off into midair. They were probably a little ashamed to confess that they had been arguing about which of them would be the greatest disciple. It's as if they were trying to guess which one of them would be the first to make the cover of *Time* magazine, and how they could get there.

These disciples were neither the first nor the last to wonder how they could achieve greatness. The world has plenty of answers to that question. Hollywood answers it by handing out the Oscars. The greatest is the one who earns the praise of his or her peers. The way to greatness is the way of fame and applause.

Donald Trump also has an answer. The greatest is the one with the most and best of everything. The way to greatness is the way of amassing wealth, property, and possessions.

Polarizing politicians have their answer. The ones who are greatest are the ones who amass political power, influence, and control. The way to greatness is the way of coercion and the defeat of anyone who dares to get in the way.

The "prosperity gospel" preachers have their answer. The greatest are those who can manipulate the power of God to get what they want; greatness is getting God to do what we want God to do.

The disciples' egocentric little debate created the opportunity for Jesus to define his own, very peculiar way to greatness. Jesus said, "Whoever wants to be first must be last of all and servant of all" (Mark 9:35).

Talk about a radical renovation! It's no wonder the disciples didn't get it. It was so odd, so outside the box of the world's expectations, so contradictory to their cultural assumptions, that it went right over their heads.

James and John clearly didn't get it. You have to respect their nerve. They don't even ask Jesus a question; they just announce what they want like a demanding customer in a discount department store. "Teacher, we want you to do for us whatever we ask of you" (Mark 10:35).

Wouldn't that be great? Wouldn't it be great if we could get Jesus to do whatever we want? Wouldn't it be great if we could unleash divine power to accomplish our goals? Wouldn't it be great if we could get God on our side so that our church, our nation, our business, our political party, and our basketball team always come out on top? Wouldn't it be great if we could sing "God Bless America" not as a plea for God's grace, but as a demand for God's support? Wouldn't it be great to get Jesus to do whatever we ask?

Jesus plays along with them by asking, "What is it you want me to do?" James and John knew what they wanted. They could see it on the horizon: "Grant us to sit, one at your right hand and one at your left, in your glory" (Mark 10:36-37).

I've always identified with these guys. My name is James. My twin brother is named John. The idea of being on the right and left hand of Jesus doesn't sound so bad to me. But then I remember that Mark uses that phrase "one at your right hand and one at your left" again in Mark 15:27 when he writes, "And with him [Jesus] they crucified two bandits, one on his right and one on his left." Mark knows what it will mean to be on the right and on the left of Jesus. It will mean being with him at the cross. But these guys, James and John, just don't get it. Neither do we.

Jesus replies to their audacious request with that haunting question, "Are you able to drink the cup that I drink?" And the disciples naively reply, "We are able" (Mark 10:38, 39).

I can't read those words without wandering back in my memory to the Methodist youth camps that I attended as a teenager. I can still hear us singing those words in commitment services in "The Green Cathedral" at Wesley Woods or beneath the hillside cross at Jumonville. The verse begins with Jesus' question:

"Are ye able," said the Master,
"to be crucified with me?"
"Yea," the sturdy dreamers answered,
"to the death we follow thee."

Then, with all the lusty naïveté of adolescent spirituality, we'd sing the refrain at the top of our lungs:

Lord, we are able. Our spirits are thine.
Remold them, make us, like thee, divine.
Thy guiding radiance above us shall be
a beacon to God, to love, and loyalty.
(Earl Marlatt, "Are Ye Able"; 1926)

It's a stirring old hymn. But sometimes when I sing that refrain I think I can hear Jesus saying, "Are you sure you heard the question?" The question Jesus asks is, "Are you able to be *crucified* with me?" Am I able to follow Jesus in the way of self-giving love revealed at the cross? Am I willing to live a cross-shaped life of servanthood?

The dialogue with James and John becomes the setting in which Jesus once again defines his peculiar way to greatness:

"You know that among the Gentiles those whom they recognize as their rulers lord it over them, and their great ones are tyrants over them. But it is not so among you; but whoever wishes to become great among you must be your servant, and whoever wishes to be first among you must be slave of all. For the Son of Man came not to be served but to serve, and to give his life a ransom for many." (Mark 10:42-45)

All of the world's ways to greatness have one thing in common. They all assume that we are here to be served; that the point of life is to get what we want the way we want it. But Jesus' peculiar way to greatness begins with the assumption that we are here to serve. Jesus calls for nothing less than a fundamental reorientation of our lives. The question he forces upon us is simply this: Am I here to be served? Or am I here to serve?

Tom Fox was a member of the Christian Peacemaker Teams who chose to follow Jesus' way of nonviolence as a witness for peace in Iraq. He was kidnapped, held hostage, and ultimately murdered. In October 2004, he wrote in his blog from Baghdad:

> It seems easier somehow to confront anger within my heart than it is to confront fear. But if Jesus and Gandhi are right then I am not to give in to either. . . . I am asked to risk my life and if I lose it to be as forgiving as they were when murdered by the forces of Satan. I struggle to stand firm but I'm willing to keep working at it. (http://waitingin thelight.blogspot.com/2004_10_01_waitinginthelight_archive.html)

Tom Fox got it. He understood Jesus' radical way of servanthood. The problem with that kind of heroic witness is that most of us will not go to Baghdad, and most of us will not be martyrs for the faith. Most of us are called to live a life of servanthood in very ordinary, often mundane, sometimes boring places.

My wife is part of a team of women from our church who drive for Meals on Wheels. Their route takes them into the housing projects and ramshackle homes in one of the poorest neighborhoods of our city. One woman on the team has been driving this route for nearly twenty years. These volunteers know each person they serve by name. They know their stories. They serve each one with a sense of dignity and respect that is a clear witness that they have been called to this ministry as a servant of others. And in the process, they have been changed. When I see the way they care about the people they serve, I think they are getting it.

Every Sunday morning, over 100 homeless people come to our

church for a hot breakfast. I'm grateful for the difference this ministry makes in the lives of hungry men and women. But I'm even more grateful for the difference it is making the lives of those who serve them. I think they are getting it.

When I see the looks on the faces of persons who have found a way to serve others, I remember the words of Albert Schweitzer: "I don't know what your destiny will be, but one thing I know: the only ones among you who will be really happy are those who will have sought and found how to serve" (quoted in *Returning: A Spiritual Journey* [New York: Doubleday, 1988] page 201).

When I see the radical renovation that happens in the lives of ordinary people through their experience of servanthood, I know that they got it!

Questions for Discussion and Reflection

1. What is your definition of *greatness*? Explain your reasoning. *Someone committed to worthy cause*
2. In what ways can you identify with James and John in the Gospel story from Mark? *Human natures wants us to do the right thing but how long will we last?*
3. When have you experienced "being served" in a really great way? What did the person serving you do? How did it feel to be served? *meals after having a baby – volunteer babysitting*
4. When have you experienced being a servant? What did you do? How did you feel?
5. What are some of the ordinary places in which you can model the servanthood of Jesus? *School or at job – to family neighbor*

Prayer

O Master, let me walk with Thee,
In lowly paths of service free;
Tell me Thy secret; help me bear
The strain of toil, the fret of care.

Teach me Thy patience; still with Thee
In closer, dearer, company,
In work that keeps faith sweet and strong,
In trust that triumphs over wrong.

23

In hope that sends a shining ray
Far down the future's broadening way,
In peace that only Thou canst give,
With Thee, O Master, let me live.
(Washington Gladden, 1879)

Focus for the Week

Jesus' way to greatness is the way of serving rather than being served.

Surrender: Nothing Short of Everything

Scripture: Read Luke 18:18-34, 19:1-10.

March 25, 2007, marked the 200th anniversary of the implementation of the Act of Parliament that abolished the slave trade in Great Britain. Filmmakers acknowledged the anniversary by releasing the movie *Amazing Grace*. The movie told the story by painting dramatic portraits of William Wilberforce, who led the movement, and John Newton, the former slave-ship captain who bore witness to the radical renovation of his life by writing the hymn "Amazing grace, how sweet the sound, that saved a wretch like me." The National Portrait Gallery in London marked the anniversary with an exhibit that brought together the portraits of those who suffered under slavery, those who profited by it, and those who led the movement to end it.

Luke is the patron saint of artists and sculptors. In the scripture readings for this week Luke brought together the portraits of two people who met Jesus at a critical turning point in their lives. By seeing the radical renovation Jesus brought in their lives, we can see another part of the radical renovation that God intends to do in our own.

The man in the first portrait is anonymous. Though no one caught his name, no one could forget him, either. Matthew, Mark, and Luke all told his story. Mark simply calls him "a man." Luke identifies him as "a certain ruler." Matthew says he was young. All agree that he was rich. As a result, he's remembered as "the rich young ruler." He had wealth, he had power, and he had youth. Position, power, possessions; those are the big three, and this guy had them all. By the world's standards, he had everything going for him.

I really like this guy. My guess is that you'd like him, too. One commentary says, "He represents wealthy, successful young people whom Matthew's church would like to attract, but who often were uninterested in the different value system by which the Christian community lived" (*The People's New Testament Commentary* [Louisville, Ky.: Westminster John Knox Press, 2004], page 78). Those are the people my church would like to reach, too. I picture this man from Luke 18:18-30 as one of the young, well-educated, type-A personality, high achievers on *The Apprentice*.

We also discover that he was a faithful, synagogue-attending, rule-keeping sort of guy. When Jesus gave him an exam on the Ten Commandments, he replied, "I have kept all these since my youth" (verse 21), which was more than could be said for most of the crowd Jesus was hanging out with and is probably more than we can say about ourselves. Everyone knew this young man was a very good man.

One more thing we know about him is that he was spiritually bankrupt. With everything he had, he also had a deep inner longing for something more. He came running to Jesus and fell on his knees as he asked, "Good Teacher, what must I do to inherit eternal life?" (Luke 18:18). He was looking for "life that really is life" (1 Timothy 6:19). He wanted to find the kind of life he had seen in Jesus, life that would be so alive with the presence of God that it could never be put to death.

I know folks like that. By the world's standards, they have it all, but they are empty on the inside, hollow to the core, always searching for the next thrill, grasping for the next rung on the ladder, wanting something they haven't found. All sorts of people in all sorts of ways are asking, How do I find life that really is life?

I've known folks in the church who are like this man. They keep the rules; they come to worship; they sing the hymns; they recite the creed; they are good people. In fact, they are boringly good, tediously religious, and tragically unhappy. They've kept the rules, but they've never experienced the joy, vitality, and power of real life flowing through their veins. Like this rich young ruler, they are searching for a "radical renovation" in the way they live.

I *like* this guy, but Mark says that Jesus *loved* him; loved him with the infinite, saving love of God; loved him so much that he wanted him to find what he was looking for; loved him enough to go to the cross to save him.

All three of those Gospels, Matthew, Mark, and Luke, say that Jesus "looked at him." Just the way a cardiologist looks into a person's heart to find the blockage that is stopping the flow of blood, Jesus looked into this guy's soul to find what was blocking the flow of God's life into his life. Jesus found it. All three Gospel writers recorded the diagnosis: "There is still one thing lacking. Sell all that you own and distribute the money to the poor, and you will have treasure in heaven; then come, follow me" (Luke 18:22).

One thing kept this guy from living the life of the kingdom of God. One thing blocked the flow of God's life in his experience. One thing stood in the way of the salvation this guy so deeply desired: it was his wealth.

The problem was not that he had riches, but that his riches had *him*. He was possessed by his possessions; he was in slavery to his position, possessions, and power. For this guy, salvation meant being set free from his bondage to his possessions.

My guess is that selling his possessions to give to the poor was not exactly what this guy had in mind when he came to Jesus. It was the last thing he expected to hear and the last thing he was capable of surrendering. Mark says that when he heard this, "he was shocked and went away grieving, for he had many possessions" (Mark 10:22). Here's the way Eugene Peterson paraphrases that in *The Message*:

> The man's face clouded over. This was the last thing he expected to hear, and he walked off with a heavy heart. He was holding on tight to a lot of things, and not about to let go.

This blew the disciples' minds. I imagine them thinking, *What are you doing, Jesus? This is just the kind of guy we need. He could bring some status and prestige to this motley crew, and we could really use his money!* But Jesus let him walk away. Then he explained the problem to the disciples.

> Jesus looked at him and said, "How hard it is for those who have wealth to enter the kingdom of God! Indeed, it is easier for a camel to

go through the eye of a needle than for someone who is rich to enter the kingdom of God." (Luke 18:24-25)

Growing up in the church, I heard lots of preachers say that Jesus was referring to a small gate in the Jerusalem city wall known as "the needle's eye." It was so small that merchants had to unload everything from their camels' backs so that they could crawl through on their knees. It's a marvelous homiletical device and a powerful symbol of what this story could mean in our lives, but there's no archaeological evidence that the little gate ever existed. Some scholars say that it was the invention of medieval theologians.

Jesus was using hilarious hyperbole to make the point. He was saying, "You want to know how hard it is for people who possess so much to realize that they possess nothing? You want to know how hard it is for people whose lives are cluttered with so many things to reorient their lives around the values of the kingdom of God? Just try squeezing a camel through the eye of a needle, then you'll know how hard it is."

Jesus was describing how difficult it is for all of us to surrender who and what we are in order to become what God wants us to be; to surrender what we possess in order to receive what we most deeply need; to surrender the one thing that blocks the flow of God's life into our lives. Here's the way Peterson paraphrases the disciples' response:

> *That* set the disciples back on their heels. "Then who has any chance at all?" they asked. Jesus was blunt: "No chance at all if you think you can pull it off by yourself. Every chance in the world if you let God do it." (Mark 10:26-27, *The Message*)

There must have been an uncomfortable silence while this guy wrestled with his decision. Then Luke records, "When he heard this"—what Jesus was asking of him—"he became sad; for he was very rich" (Luke 18:23). The scene is even more poignant in Matthew: "When the young man heard this word, he went away grieving, for he had many possessions" (Matthew 19:22). The rich young ruler walked away grieving. I'll bet Jesus was grieving, too. We never hear of this guy again. In the end, he is lost. We have his portrait, but we don't even know his name.

28

Every kid in Sunday school knows the name and the story of the man in the second portrait in Luke's gallery. In fact, they can sing it:

Zacchaeus was a wee little man
And a wee little man was he
He climbed up in a sycamore tree
For the Lord he wanted to see
And as the Savior passed that way
He looked up in that tree
And He said, "Zacchaeus, you come down!
For I'm going to your house today
For I'm going to your house to stay."

If the rich young ruler was like a contestant on *The Apprentice*, Zacchaeus must have been a Palestinian version of Danny DeVito. But aside from being "a wee little man," what else do we know about him?

Luke says he was a chief tax collector in Jericho, one of the commercial centers of the region, which means that he was rich. It also means he was corrupt. The difference between the rich young ruler and Zacchaeus was that Zacchaeus was not a good man. He had not kept the commandments. Just doing his job he was breaking a bunch of them. Any Jew who became a tax collector was automatically excluded from the synagogue, cut off from the community of faith. Everyone knew that Zacchaeus was not a good man.

We also know that like the young man, Zacchaeus was searching for something his money could not buy. He was so spiritually bankrupt that he was willing to humiliate himself by running through town and climbing up into a sycamore tree to get a look at Jesus. His actions reflected the total abandonment of his position, power, and self-respect.

We also know that in contrast to the rich young ruler, Zacchaeus found what he was looking for. Luke says that Jesus looked at Zacchaeus, just the way he looked at the rich young ruler. To him, Jesus said, "Zacchaeus, hurry and come down; for I must stay at your house today" (19:5). Luke says that Zacchaeus "hurried down and was happy to welcome him" (verse 6). Set free from the slavery of his wealth, Zacchaeus said, "Look, half of my possessions, Lord, I will give to the poor; and if I have defrauded anyone of anything, I will pay back four times as much" (verse 8). As they headed off for

Rich young man 29 - sell everything
Zacchaeus - half of my possessions

dinner, Jesus said, "Today salvation has come to this house. . . . For the Son of Man came to seek out and to save the lost" (Luke 19:9-10).

So, why does Luke hang these two portraits so close together in the Gospel? My guess is that he wants us to see just how much they have in common with each other and with us.

First, both men were searching for life that only Jesus could give. They were searching for salvation. Both men needed to be saved, set free, liberated from the one thing that kept them from experiencing eternal life and following Jesus.

Second, both of these guys were drawn to Jesus. People still are. The misguided fascination with things like *The Da Vinci Code* points to the fact that there is something about Jesus that never ceases to intrigue, captivate, disturb, pester, and challenge us.

Third, both of these guys met Jesus in the practical, tangible, ordinary stuff of their lives. In the Bible, salvation is not some ethereal, otherworldly, spooky thing. Salvation has to do with the real, tangible stuff of our very real lives. Salvation is being set free from the one thing that keeps us from following Jesus.

For these guys, that "one thing" was their position, power, and possessions. Their attitude toward their wealth kept them from following Jesus.

I'd like to tell you that this story isn't really about money, wealth, and possessions, but it really is, because the Bible knows that our attitude toward our possessions is often the one thing that is most likely to get in the way of our obedience to Christ. It's often the one thing that keeps us from living the cross-shaped life.

The story is about money, but it isn't *only* about money. The one thing that blocks the flow of God's life in your life could be something else.

It might be pride, power, prestige, or position.

It might be self-destructive addictions.

It might be the memory of past hurts and emotional abuse; a victim mentality that keeps us from claiming the gift of life.

It might be overcommitment to our career that keeps us from healthy relationships in the rest of our lives.

It might be racial, cultural, or political prejudice.

It might be the way you use your time, energy, or resources, the places you go, the things you do, the sites you visit on the Internet.

I don't know what that "one thing" is for you, but Jesus loves each of us enough to look deeply into our souls and lead us to the one thing that needs to be surrendered to the love of God at the cross.

Fourth, both of these guys were given a choice. The rich young ruler went home sad and lost. Zacchaeus went home happy and saved.

Those choices come to us, too. Sometimes they come in dramatic, life-altering moments that mark a radical change of direction for our lives. But most of the time they come in the ordinary, practical, seemingly insignificant daily decisions that shape our obedience to Christ.

When I referred to this story in my weekly online message to our congregation, one person responded by reminding me of the words of C. S. Lewis.

> Every time you make a choice you are turning the central part of you, the part of you that chooses, into something a little different from what it was before. And taking your life as a whole, with all your innumerable choices, all your life long you are slowly turning this central thing either into a heavenly creature or into a hellish creature: either into a creature that is in harmony with God, and with its fellow creature, and with itself, or else into one that is in a state of war and hatred with God, and with its fellow creatures, and with itself. . . . Each of us at each moment is progressing to the one state or the other. (*Mere Christianity* [New York: Touchstone, 1980], page 87)

The person writing the response added: "Talk about a turning point! It's a constant part of life as we continue to choose in even the most minor of ways."

I think Luke hangs these two portraits together to force the question upon every one of us: Will we be like the rich young ruler, who turned and walked away sad? Or will we be like Zacchaeus, who, Luke said, "was happy to welcome him" and who heard Jesus say, "Today salvation has come to this house."

Questions for Reflection and Discussion

1. Use a hymnal or some other source to locate the words to the hymn "Amazing Grace." Read the words carefully and reflect upon them. How does God's gift of amazing grace touch you personally?

31

2. Describe the rich young ruler as you picture him. In what ways can you identify with him? *it is easier to stay in a comfortable place*
3. In what ways are you like Zacchaeus? How do you picture him?
4. What is the "one thing" that stands in the way of your obedience to Christ? *fear of change*
5. What would it mean for you to hear Jesus say, "Today salvation has come to this house"?

Prayer

All to Jesus I surrender;
all to him I freely give;
I will ever love and trust him,
in his presence daily live.

All to Jesus I surrender;
humbly at his feet I bow,
worldly pleasures all forsaken;
take me, Jesus, take me now.

. . . .

All to Jesus I surrender;
now I feel the sacred flame.
O the joy of full salvation!
Glory, glory to his name!

Refrain:
I surrender all, I surrender all,
all to thee, my blessed Savior,
I surrender all.

("I Surrender All," J. W. Van Deventer, 1896)

Focus for the Week

What is the one thing that stands in the way of the new life that Christ wants to bring in my life? Am I willing to surrender that one thing to him?

Love: The Radical Center

Scripture: Read Mark 12:28-34; 1 John 4:7-21.

Here's an interesting piece of presidential trivia. The President who served the shortest time in office was William Henry Harrison, our ninth President. He was inaugurated in 1841 and served for just thirty-two days. Harrison also takes the prize for delivering the longest inaugural address in history. It went on for one hour and forty-five minutes. He delivered all 8,445 words in a snowstorm, immediately caught pneumonia, and died a month later. There's no record of how many people who sat through the speech may have suffered the same fate. By contrast, Lincoln's Gettysburg Address, with only 267 words, stands out as one of the most formative addresses in our nation's history.

What can you say about William Henry Harrison? You might say that he spent most of his presidency talking about it. Or you might say that he is remembered more for the number of his words than the number of his accomplishments. Or you might say that words are cheap unless they result in action. Or you could say the words of Ralph Waldo Emerson that I saw on the wall of the Great Hall in the Library of Congress: "Words are also actions and actions are a kind of words." Or you could say what the writer of the first epistle of John said: "Little children, let us love, not in word or speech, but in truth and action" (1 John 3:18).

The radical renovation that God is at work to accomplish in our lives is not just a matter of words or talk; it is about truth and action.

33

Love is the action by which God's reconstruction of us is accomplished. Love defined by the life, death, and resurrection of Jesus Christ is not so much something we *feel* as it is something we *do*. The love with which God loves us and the love we are called to share with others is not just love in word or speech. It is love in truth and in action. It is love that is shaped by the cross.

During these weeks of Lent we've been thinking about the radical work of interior renovation that God wants to accomplish in and through us. The Bible says that God intends a total reorientation of our sin-distorted lives and a complete reconstruction of this sin-damaged world. It is nothing less than a radical reconstruction of cosmic proportions. This week we come to the irreducible core of that new life, the fundamental redesign of our living, the motivating center of Christian discipleship that drives and influences everything else.

A religious scholar asked Jesus, "What is the greatest, the first, the most important of all the commandments?" (Mark 12:28, author's paraphrase). In answering this question, Jesus reached back to the foundation of Hebrew faith.

> "The first is, 'Hear, O Israel: the Lord our God, the Lord is one; you shall love the Lord your God with all your heart, and with all your soul, and with all your mind, and with all your strength.' The second is this, 'You shall love your neighbor as yourself.' There is no other commandment greater than these." (Mark 12:29-31)

There was nothing new about those commandments. Jesus was quoting familiar words straight out of the Old Testament. (See Deuteronomy 6:4 and Leviticus 19:18.) The unique thing is the way Jesus bound two separate statements together. Jesus said that the greatest of the commandments is the combination of love for God—the kind of love that involves the whole of our being, our mind, our heart, our soul, and our strength—and love for others—the kind of love that takes action on behalf of another.

"You shall love the Lord your God" means that cross-shaped love begins not with us, but with God. We don't begin with our human understanding of love and define God by it; we begin with God's great act of love in Jesus Christ and define our understanding of love by it. The love that God defines is not, as a popular movie advertisement declared, "a force of nature." Lust is a force of nature; love is a choice. The love that God defines is love in action, love that chooses to give itself away for someone else. It's at the core of the gospel: "God loved the world so much that he *gave* his only-begotten son" (John 3:16, author's paraphrase). The epistle of John says,

> We love because [God] first loved us. . . . In this is love, not that we loved God but that he loved us and sent his Son to be the atoning sacrifice for our sins. (1 John 4:19, 10)

Here's just how radical the love of God is.

You are loved so much by God that Jesus died for you.

Your family members, even the most irritating of them, are loved so much by God that Jesus died for them.

Your neighbors, even the ones who drive you crazy, are loved so much by God that Jesus died for them.

Democrats are loved so much by God that Jesus died for them.

Republicans are loved so much by God that Jesus died for them.

Israelis and Palestinians are loved so much by God that Jesus died for them.

Osama bin Laden is loved so much by God that Jesus died for him.

Saddam Hussein was loved so much by God that Jesus died for him.

God loved every human being in this whole broken world so much that God gave his only Son for them.

Cross-shaped love begins with God's act of love in Jesus Christ, and then, on the basis of what God has done for us, we are called to actively love others. "Beloved," John said, "since God loved us so much, we also ought to love one another" (1 John 4:11).

John could hardly make the point more clearly.

> Those who say, "I love God," and hate their brothers or sisters, are liars; for those who do not love a brother or sister whom they have seen, cannot love God whom they have not seen. The commandment we have from him is this: those who love God must love their brothers and sisters also. (1 John 4:20-21)

Love God with all your heart and soul and mind and strength. And love every person you meet with cross-shaped love. This, Jesus said, is the first and greatest commandment. When we act for others in self-giving love, Jesus said we are not far from the kingdom of God. When we act in Christlike love, we become the answer to the prayer, "Your kingdom come, your will be done on earth as it is in heaven."

God is at work to renovate our lives and reconstruct our world through active, self-giving love. When we demonstrate that love in tangible action, we participate in the coming of the kingdom of God. Every individual act of love undermines the power of evil, violence, hatred, and sin in this world and becomes a part of God's great, saving love for the whole creation.

Martin Luther King, Jr., taught and demonstrated the transformative power of Christlike love. In his classic sermon "An Experiment in Love," he wrote, "To meet hate with retaliatory hate would do nothing but intensify the existence of evil in the universe. Hate begets hate; violence begets violence; toughness begets a greater toughness. We must meet the forces of hate with the power of love" (*A Testament of Hope* [New York: Harper & Row, 1986], page 17). He was absolutely convinced that love is "the most durable power in the world" (page 11).

Twice during the years I've been in the ministry I had the privilege of serving neighboring congregations with the Reverend George Carlton. For a young preacher, George was the model of a Christlike pastor, a consistently gracious, genuinely loving man who treated every person with a profound sense of dignity and compassion. He offered a genuine gift of love to everyone who met him. I knew all of that about George, but it was not until his death that I heard about a pivotal moment that became a part of God's call on his life.

George was born in Wauchula, Florida, and was only sixteen years old when he enlisted in the U.S. Army in 1942. At the age of eighteen he went ashore with the troops on D-Day, and he was injured twice before being captured behind enemy lines in 1945.

He and his fellow POWs were forced to march hundreds of miles as they moved from camp to camp on daily rations that consisted of a small piece of bread and some watery potato soup. George lost sixty pounds during his captivity. One day, as they were marching through a small German town, a German woman risked her life when she ran up to him and, in an act of unexpected love, thrust a warm loaf of bread into George's hands.

It was just a loaf of bread; just one, unexpected, anonymous act of self-giving love on the part of a nameless German woman who never spoke a word. But for George, it would become an act of self-giving love that would influence the rest of his life. He spent the rest of his life offering that gift of love to others.

Beloved, let us love, not in word or in speech, but in truth and in action, because loving God and loving others is the greatest commandment of all.

Questions for Reflection or Discussion

1. What does the word love mean to you? Is it something you feel or something you do? Explain your reasoning.
2. What difference does it make for you to define love not by what *you* do, but by what God has done in Christ?
3. How have you experienced God's love in your life?
4. How have you demonstrated the love of God in your actions?
5. Who do you know who models loving God and loving others in their actions? Describe this person or these persons.

Prayer

O Love that wilt not let me go,
I rest my weary soul in thee;
I give thee back the life I owe,
that in thine ocean depths
its flow may richer, fuller be.

. . . .

O Joy that seekest me through pain,
I cannot close my heart to thee;
I trace the rainbow through the rain,
and feel the promise is not vain,
that morn shall tearless be.

O Cross that liftest up my head,
I dare not ask to fly from thee;
I lay in dust life's glory dead,

and from the ground there blossoms
red life that shall endless be.

(George Matheson, "O Love That Wilt Not Let Me Go"; 1882)

Focus for the Week

The love that God defines is demonstrated in what we do more than in what we say.

Reconciliation: Something That Doesn't Love a Wall

Scripture: Read Ephesians 2:12-22.

I t's just a little chunk of concrete. It looks a lot like any chunk of concrete you could pick up around any construction site in the city. But this one is different, because this little chunk of concrete came from the Berlin Wall.

Some of us remember August 13, 1961, the day the wall went up, dividing the world into East and West. Some of us remember June 26, 1963, the day John F. Kennedy stood in front of that wall and declared, "I am a Berliner," though the "urban legend" is that some people thought they heard him say, "I am a jelly doughnut." Some of us remember June 12, 1987, when President Ronald Reagan, addressing the leader of the Soviet Union and referring to the Berlin Wall, said, "Mr. Gorbachev, tear down this wall." And who will forget November 9, 1989, the day the wall came down?

A reporter for *The Orlando Sentinel* chipped a little chunk out of the wall five days later and brought it back for me. It's the tangible witness to the truth of the lines from Robert Frost that I borrowed for the title of this chapter. They come from his poem "Mending Wall" (1915):

Something there is that doesn't love a wall,
That sends the frozen-ground-swell under it,

And spills the upper boulders in the sun;
And makes gaps even two can pass abreast.

. . . .

Something there is that doesn't love a wall,
That wants it down.

When the Christians in Ephesus heard Paul's words about "the dividing wall" of hostility, they could have pictured another wall. It was just as real, just as hard, just as impenetrable as the Berlin Wall. It was the wall in the Temple in Jerusalem that separated the outer court, where Gentiles were permitted, from the inner court that was open only to Jews. Archaeologists have found the inscriptions, written in Greek, that were placed along that wall. They read, "No outsider shall enter the protective enclosure around the sanctuary. Whoever is caught will only have himself to blame for the ensuing death."

Not exactly what you would call "Southern hospitality," is it? It makes me wonder what kind of invisible inscriptions are carved on the walls around our churches, our homes, and our lives. What are some of the unspoken barriers that prevent people from experiencing the love of God and becoming disciples of Jesus Christ through our lives?

The dividing walls we construct may be very subtle, but they are no less real.

A member of our church staff who possesses the gift of hospitality told me about seeing a woman coming onto the church property who was obviously frustrated and confused. When this member of the staff asked if he could help, the woman told him what a difficult time she had finding a place to park. When she finally got parked, she couldn't find her way to the sanctuary. The staff member pointed her in the right direction and then wondered what would happen if she stepped through the lobby door and no one helped her find a seat, or if, God forbid, she accidentally sat in someone else's favorite pew! What would it take for her to be able to experience God's presence in worship given all that she had been through? The result was his leadership of a hospitality team to meet people in the parking lot and help them find their way.

A quiet, gentle guy from Puerto Rico shared with me what happened to him one Sunday when the usher at the sanctuary door misunderstood something he said because of his accent. In what was probably an attempt to be friendly, the usher tried to turn the misunderstanding into a joke, but it wasn't funny. It left the Puerto Rican man feeling like an outsider in the congregation.

Christlike hospitality is about tearing down the walls that prevent people from experiencing God's love. It's about loving people enough to clear away the subtle barriers that block the flow of the Spirit of Christ into their lives.

Back to the scripture text, Paul, writing to the Ephesians, makes this all very personal. The apostle's words force us to ask, "What are the dividing walls in my life?"

One Sunday when I preached on this text, I invited my congregation to join me in an exercise in group-confession. I invited them to respond with the words "Lord, have mercy" if any of these petitions applied to their lives:

> If you have ever felt estranged from another person because he or she was better looking, better dressed, had a better job, lived in a better house, or drove a better car than you do, let us pray to the Lord, *Lord, have mercy.*

> If you have ever thought that Florida would be a dandy place to live if we could just get rid of all those tourists, Midwest retirees, or teenage drivers, let us pray to the Lord, *Lord, have mercy.*

> If you have ever felt alienated from another person solely because that person was rich, poor, black, white, Hispanic, Haitian, Republican, Democrat, or because he or she cheered for a rival football team, let us pray to the Lord, *Lord, have mercy.*

> If you have ever had a night when it felt like the bed in which you and your spouse were sleeping was about ten feet wide; if you've ever felt that your parents were out to destroy your life, or your kids were determined to ruin your retirement, let us pray to the Lord, *Lord, have mercy.*

> If you've ever been so alone that you felt as if you were an alien, a stranger, having no hope, without God in the world, let us pray to the Lord, *Lord, have mercy.*

In one way or another, we've all been up against that wall. We've pushed against it, written graffiti on it, or scratched the surface of it.

Sometimes we've cursed it, sometimes we've hidden in its shadows, and sometimes we secretly loved it because it protected us from facing people we didn't want to meet.

But something is there that doesn't love a wall . . . that wants it down! And that something is the loving, redeeming, saving power of the almighty God.

> In Christ Jesus you who once were far off have been brought near by the blood of Christ. For he is our peace; in his flesh he has made both groups into one and has broken down the dividing wall, that is, the hostility between us . . . that he might create in himself one new humanity in place of the two, thus making peace, and might reconcile both groups to God in one body through the cross. (Ephesians 2:13-16)

The gospel declares that God's way of breaking down the walls that divide us from each other and separate us from God is not the way of force or violence or intimidation or war. Violence may enable you to kill your enemy, but it will never transform your enemy into a friend. War may be able to end a conflict, but it will never build a community.

God's way of breaking down the walls of hostility is the way of redemptive love; specifically, the self-giving, dying love of God revealed at the cross. It is the way of the One who comes to alienated, divided, separated, lonely people, and through the costly love of Jesus draws us out of our isolation, out of our hostility, out of our loneliness, and into a whole new humanity, into one body shaped by the cross.

At the turn of the twentieth century, Edwin Markham wrote these lines, perhaps out of the brokenness in his own experience:

> He drew a circle that shut me out—
> Heretic, rebel, a thing to flout.
> But Love and I had the wit to win:
> We drew a circle that took him in!
> (*Modern American Poetry* [New York: Harcourt, Brace & World, 1962], page 106)

It isn't easy. The process of redemption is hard work—as hard as going to the cross. It doesn't happen all at once. It will, in its own way, be just as costly for us as it was for Jesus. But it can happen. And it does happen. The walls can come down, and a new humanity can be born.

We heard it in the words and saw it in the life of Martin Luther King, Jr., who called us to move beyond retribution to reconciliation, beyond conflict into community.

We heard it in the words and saw it in the lives of Desmond Tutu and Nelson Mandela, who led their people out of hatred into hope, out of injustice and toward a common destiny in a new nation.

I've heard it in the words and seen it in the lives of alienated couples who—through the hard, costly work of love—have found forgiveness, healing, and a new relationship.

I've heard it in the words and seen it in the lives of family members, neighbors, and fellow church members who, after years of alienation, were brought back into relationship with each other through a combination of hard work and great grace.

A woman told me the story of the walls she had built around her life. Because of the pain, rejection, and abuse she had experienced as a child, she built a protective wall around herself in an attempt to protect her from more pain. She had not been inside a church in years when she showed up in our congregation and began to experience something of the love of God. She decided to try one of our small groups. She said that the first time she walked into the room she felt like an alien, alone, different in many ways from the rest of the people in the group. She walked out of the room that night not sure that she would return, but she came back again, and again, and again, and by the time the group's study series was completed, she had been drawn into a whole new sense of community with every person in that room. The walls, if not broken down, had at least been cracked open, and she had begun to walk through.

Her story is a living example of the bold affirmation that Paul offers to each of us.

So then you are no longer strangers and aliens, but you are citizens with the saints and also members of the household of God, built upon the foundation of the apostles and prophets, with Christ Jesus himself as the cornerstone. In him the whole structure is joined together and grows into a holy temple in the Lord; in whom you also are built together spiritually into a dwelling place for God. (Ephesians 2:19-22)

There is something that doesn't love a wall, and that something is the love of God revealed at the cross. We can choose to build walls or to build a dwelling place for God. Which will you choose?

Questions for Reflection and Discussion

1. Robert Frost's poem "Mending Wall" paints a picture of one farmer building a stone wall to separate his field from his neighbor's field. How does that poetic image speak to you? You may wish to find and read the entire poem.
2. What are some of the dividing walls that you have experienced in your life? Who was on the other side? How was the wall constructed? Who built it?
3. Reread Ephesians 2:11-16. What difference does the death of Jesus on the cross make in the way you relate to other people?
4. How have you been "brought near by the blood of Christ" (Ephesians 2:13)? What does it mean for you to say that Jesus has "made both groups into one and has broken down the dividing wall, that is, the hostility between us" (Ephesians 2:14)? Where have you seen Christ creating a "new humanity" through the blood of the cross (Ephesians 2:15)?
5. Reread Ephesians 2:19-22. What would need to change for your church to fulfill the apostle Paul's vision?

Prayer

Almighty God, who has broken down every wall of division by your love at the cross, forgive us for continuing to build walls that separate us from others. Help us accept each other as you have accepted us in your grace. At the foot of the cross, teach us to live and love in the way of Jesus that as one new humanity, we may know the joy and fullness of your love. Amen.

Focus for the Week

The love of God at the cross breaks down every barrier and unites us in a new humanity in Christ.

Sacrifice: It's Nothing if It Costs Nothing

Scripture: Read Mark 14:1-19.

The economic extravagance of the woman's action simply blew everyone who saw it away. The perfume she poured on Jesus' feet was high quality, pure nard, shipped in from India, worth at least 300 *denarii*, which was equal to the annual salary of a common worker. It was the kind of treasure a woman would hoard away as her financial security for the future. But this woman squandered it—just poured it out like water. Economically, her action made no sense at all.

The early Christians could never forget *what* she did, but they never agreed on *who* she was or *where* she did it. In fact, each Gospel reshaped her story to fit its own theological purpose.

John placed the story in Bethany, in the home of Lazarus, whom Jesus had just raised from the dead. (See John 12:1-8.) He identified the woman as Lazarus's sister, Mary. We financially responsible, economically conservative, balance-the-checkbook types can almost excuse her extravagance as an unrestrained expression of love for the one who brought her brother back to life.

Luke placed the story in Galilee, in the home of a Pharisee named Simon. (See Luke 7:36-50.) He didn't identify the woman, but he said that she was "a woman in the city, who was a sinner" (7:37). That description has led to a lot of salacious sermonic speculation about

45

the exact nature of her sinning, usually beginning and ending with sex. Parenthetically, have you ever wondered why most of us are more curious about sin than about goodness? Why does evil seem so enticing while goodness seems boring? And why does our curiosity about sin usually begin with sex? Those questions will have to wait for another time.

In A.D. 591, Pope Gregory I identified the woman in Luke's account as Mary Magdalene, which led to the assumption that Mary Magdalene was a prostitute. Unfortunately for Mary, that is just as unsubstantiated as *The DaVinci Code* claim that she was Jesus' wife. Finally, in 1969, someone in the Vatican declared that Pope Gregory had gotten it wrong, and the Roman Catholic Church overruled him, but the rumors about Mary still go on. Whoever she was and whatever her sin, Luke explains her action as an extravagant expression of gratitude for the forgiveness of her sin.

That brings us to Mark and Matthew, both of whom set the story in Bethany, in the home of Simon the leper (see Matthew 26:6-13; Mark 14:3-9), but neither of whom left a clue as to who this woman was or what precipitated her action. She just walks in from nowhere. Without a word of explanation, she breaks open her alabaster jar and pours the oil out on Jesus' head until it drips down onto his shoulders and the rich fragrance fills the place.

That's when the good, practical, responsible folks around the table go ballistic. Mark says they scolded her as they asked, "Why was this ointment wasted this way? It could have been sold and the money given to the poor."

Matthew, Mark, and Luke seem to give the disciples the benefit of the doubt that if they actually had the 300 *denarii* the ointment was worth, they would give it all to the poor. John is more skeptical. He says it was Judas who asked the question, and John goes on to say, "[Judas] said this not because he cared about the poor, but because he was a thief; he kept the common purse and used to steal what was put into it" (John 12:6).

John may be pouring it on a little bit heavy, there. He clearly wouldn't agree with the newly discovered manuscript of "The Gospel of Judas," which takes a kinder, gentler view of Judas. In this Gnostic Gospel, Judas is portrayed as assisting Jesus in accomplishing God's purpose, which is one of the reasons it was rejected from the Canon of scripture. However we interpret John's comments about Judas, I have discovered that it's easier to be generous with someone else's money than with my own. It's easier to give away money I *wish* I had than to share what I *do* have. Jesus' response says that we always have opportunities to serve the poor; we can do it anytime we wish. *Whether* we do it is the question.

Whatever the motivation of the critics, all the Gospels agree that the folks around the table were shocked, scandalized, appalled by what appeared to be an irrational, extravagant waste. But Jesus saw something else, something none of them could see, something that may, for all we know, have surprised the woman as much as it surprised her critics. He said, "She has anointed my body beforehand for its burial. Truly I tell you, wherever the good news is proclaimed in the whole world, what she has done will be told in remembrance of her" (Mark 14:8-9).

And, lo and behold, wherever the gospel has been proclaimed throughout the world, right down to this present day, what she did has in fact been told in remembrance of her. But what is in this story for us? How does the story of this woman draw the design for us of the radical renovation that God wants to do in our lives?

Let's begin by looking at the context. Mark locates this story two days before Passover. It is the last event he records before he begins the Passion narrative. It seems to me that he places it there to prepare us for what follows, just the way this woman prepared Jesus for his burial. Mark places it there as a sort of experiential window or spiritual lens through which he wants us to see the rest of the story. It's as if Mark is inviting us, as we walk through the story of the death of Jesus, to ask the questions people asked around the table that night.

Why this irrational waste?

Why this extravagant sacrifice?

Why this squandering of the life of Jesus?

The questions haunt us as we walk through the events of Holy Week.

Why the ruthless betrayal by Judas?

Why the broken bread and shared cup at the Passover table?

Why the soul-wrenching agony of Jesus' prayer in Gethsemane?

Why the vigilante-style arrest in the garden?

Why the charade of a trial before the high priest's council?

Why the painful denial by Peter?

47

Why Pilate's senseless perversion of justice and his capitulation to the trumped-up passions of the crowd?

Why trade Jesus, the peacemaker, for Barabbas, the murderer?

Why the humiliating mockery of the soldiers?

Why the sarcastic derision of those gathered around the cross?

And why, why in God's name, the only word that Mark records from the lips of Jesus on the cross, "My God, my God, why have you forsaken me?" (Mark 15:34)?

As the darkness closes in around us on Good Friday, isn't there something in us that wants to ask: "Why this waste?"

From the earliest days of the Christian church, scholars, theologians, preachers, and just ordinary faithful folks have wrestled with that question. They've done their best—and sometimes done their worst!—to find an answer, to explain the sacrifice of the cross, to calculate the mathematics of the atonement, to weave together a rational explanation for the irrational extravagance of God.

There is a place for that kind of intellectual adventure. There is a time for asking difficult questions and searching for rational answers. There is a time for mental calculation of the cost of the atonement. But Holy Week is not that time, and Golgotha is not that place. I think Mark locates this story where he does to prepare us to experience the extravagant gift of God's sacrificial love in the cross and to prepare us to offer ourselves in extravagant self-surrender to the One who dies for us.

One of the formative books in my preparation to become a preacher was Paul Scherer's classic, *The Word God Sent.* In his sermon "The Love That God Defines," the former professor of preaching at Princeton and Union seminaries said that when we define the love of God by the cross, we are saying "the costliest thing that could be said about God. . . . From morning to night [God] was trying desperately . . . to make whole again the life that men had taken up in their hands and broken into bits" ([New York: Harper & Row, 1965], pages 226–27).

The cross means that this extravagant God was willing to pay any price, to go to any length, to do anything necessary to accomplish the work of salvation, to fulfill the "radical renovation" that God intends for every one of our sin-twisted lives and for the whole sin-broken world. The cross is the costliest thing that can be said about God.

Scherer went on to say that when we define love by what God did at the cross, we are also saying "the costliest thing that can be said about us. . . . The point of the gospel is that God asks of us only what he gives" (Scherer, pages 229–30).

The only appropriate response to the extravagant sacrifice of the cross is to offer ourselves the way this woman in the Gospels offered her gift, in unrestrained, extravagant obedience to Jesus Christ. Like the sinful woman in Luke's Gospel, we are invited to fall in uncalculating humility before the One who forgives our sin. Like Mary of Bethany, we are challenged to respond in unrestrained gratitude to the One who promises to raise us to new life. Mark invites us to go beyond rational calculation or intellectual curiosity to experience the extravagant grace of God at the cross.

More than thirty years have passed, but just the way the early Christians couldn't forget that woman, I've never forgotten a Good Friday service I attended while I was in seminary. Dean Robert Traina was an exacting biblical scholar who demanded the highest level of scholarship from his students and who never settled for easy answers or glib platitudes. He was a singularly unemotional teacher who had no patience with the weak-kneed excuses of students who had not completed their assignments. He seemed to approach the Bible with the mind of an analytical scientist. But it was Good Friday afternoon and he was the preacher. I do not remember the rest of his sermon, but I will never forget that he concluded by attempting to quote the words from Charles Wesley's Passion hymn:

O Love divine, what hast thou done!
The incarnate God has died for me!
The Father's co-eternal Son bore all my sins upon the tree.
The Son of God for me has died:
My Lord, my Love, is crucified!

Like the crowd around that dinner table in Simon's house, we were all blown away when Dean Traina stopped midway through the first verse. His voice cracked. His lips quivered. We could feel the lump in his throat as he was simply overwhelmed by the sheer extravagance of God's love at the cross. There was a long, painful silence. Then, with a tear running down his cheek, he read the rest of the hymn as an invitation to each of us, which is the way I offer it to you:

Is crucified for me and you,
To bring us rebels back to God.
Believe, believe the record true,
Ye all are bought with Jesus' blood.
Pardon for all flows from his side:
My Lord, my Love, is crucified!

Behold him, all ye that pass by,
The bleeding Prince of life and peace!
Come, sinners, see your Savior die,
And say, "Was ever grief like his?"
Come, feel with me his blood applied:
My Lord, my Love, is crucified!

(Charles Wesley, "O Love Divine, What Hast Thou Done"; 1742)

Questions for Reflection and Discussion

1. What do you think might have motivated the extravagant generosity of the woman in the Gospel story? How do you picture her?
2. When have you experienced the kind of extravagance that is modeled by the woman in this story?
3. What feelings do you bring to the events of Holy Week? What are some of the most powerful memories you carry related to these stories?
4. What would it mean for you to offer yourself in extravagant love to God?
5. What do you hope to experience during Holy Week this year?

Prayer

Almighty and everliving God, in your tender love for the human race you sent your Son our Savior Jesus Christ to take upon him our nature, and to suffer death upon the cross, giving us the example of his great humility: Mercifully grant that we may walk in the way of his suffering, and also share in his resurrection; through Jesus Christ our Lord, who lives and reigns with you and the Holy Spirit, one God, for ever and ever. Amen. (*Book of Common Prayer,* 1979, page 219)

Focus for the Week

The extravagant love of God at the cross calls us to respond in extravagant love for Christ.

Hope: He Goes Before You!

So they went out and fled from the tomb, for terror and amazement had seized them; and they said nothing to anyone, for they were afraid. (Mark 16:8)

Y ou have to admit that it's a shabby way to end the Gospel. Any of us who know the other Resurrection stories could have done better. Imagine how Easter worshipers would respond if the service concluded with Mark's words and they were sent out too afraid to speak to anyone. You can't blame other early Christians for turning the sixteenth chapter of Mark into a patchwork quilt of endings, each one trying to improve on the one before it. But biblical scholars generally agree that this is where Mark left it. In Greek, it ends with a dangling preposition, a sort of a ragged nonending to the Gospel.

Thomas G. Long, who teaches preaching at Emory University's Candler School of Theology, tells the story of an actor who memorized the Gospel of Mark and presented it as a dramatic reading. At the end of the performance the audience was obviously waiting for some kind of grand finale that would bring them to their feet with the "Hallelujah" chorus. But the actor simply repeated Mark's words, stood there for an awkward moment of silence, turned, and walked off the stage. Long described "the discomfort and uncertainty within the audience" and said that the conversations in the lobby were dominated by what he called "the experience of the nonending" (*The Christian Century*, April 4, 2006; page 19). The ragged nonending of

Mark's Gospel is a little like a renovation project that is never completed; one of those home-repair projects that never seems to be done.

Sarah Winchester was the widow of William Wirt Winchester and the daughter-in-law of Oliver Winchester, the manufacturers of the Winchester Rifle, referred to as "the gun that won the West." After the death of her baby daughter and later her husband, Sarah turned to spiritualism. Legend has it that a medium convinced her that she could appease the spirits of all those who had been killed by her husband's guns as long as she continued construction on her Victorian mansion in San Jose, California. Sarah hired a construction team that worked nonstop, twenty-four hours a day for thirty-eight years. (It makes me wonder if the medium might have owned stock in the construction company!)

The 160-room mansion is full of bizarre architectural effects that, it is said, were designed to trick the spirit of death. There's a window built into the floor and another that opens into a wall. There are staircases that lead nowhere and doors that open into blank walls. All of it was an elaborate, nonstop construction project that attempted to outwit death.

We may not go to the lengths of Sarah Winchester, but most of us some of the time, and some of us most of the time, are tempted to find more subtle and less eccentric ways to live in denial of death. Have you noticed the euphemisms obituary writers often use to avoid saying that a person died? The person "entered into eternal rest," "began his eternal retirement," or, for baseball fans, "passed away into the 'Field of Dreams.'"

But Sarah Winchester found out that Death has a very good sense of direction. It finally found her, just the way it finds each of us. Her nonstop renovation project failed her, just the way our attempts to outwit death will fail us.

By contrast, Mark's nonending to the Gospel is a word of hope. I'm grateful for the way the other Gospel writers complete the story of the Resurrection, but I'm also grateful that the church included Mark in the canon with his dangling nonending, because it speaks to some of the inconclusive renovation projects in my life.

As hard as I try to put a reliable period at the end of every line, I keep ending up with a lot of dangling prepositions, too. As much as I try to bring closure, to tie things down, to make all the pieces fit, I keep ending up with a lot of loose ends in my life. As hard as I work at completing every renovation project I begin, some of them never seem to be completed. There are broken relationships that don't get healed, fears that never seem to go away, problems that remain unsolved, doubts that defy simple answers, temptations that return with disturbing regularity, visions that I may not live to see accomplished, dreams that I may not see fulfilled, dramas than never reach the final curtain.

The good news from Mark's version of the Easter story is not that we are given conclusive evidence of resurrection or a closing argument that will nail down the verdict, but that we are given hope. Mark says that "a young man" dressed in white, sitting at the entrance of the tomb like an usher waiting for the audience to leave the theater, told those frightened women: "Do not be alarmed; you are looking for Jesus of Nazareth, who was crucified. He has been raised; he is not here. . . . But go, tell his disciples and Peter that he is going ahead of you to Galilee; there you will see him" (Mark 16:6-7).

The other Gospels offer us *evidence* for the Resurrection; all Mark has to offer is hope. Hope that the Risen Christ goes before us and that we will find him, not in the tomb, not in the place of death, not in the place of broken dreams and shattered expectations, not in the reminder of our past, but out there, ahead of us, in the ordinary places of our lives, along the road that leads to the future. We celebrate Easter not to remember a resurrection in the past, but to experience the presence of the Risen Christ in the present and to follow him into the future.

During Holy Week in 2006, I heard the news on National Public Radio that William Sloane Coffin, the Vietnam-era chaplain at Yale University and later pastor at the Riverside Church in New York, had died. Coffin was as controversial as he was courageous. His life and preaching were animated by the incorrigible gift of hope. NPR played a recorded interview in which he said,

> Hope is a state of mind independent of the state of the world. If your heart is full of hope, you can be persistent when you can't be optimistic. You can keep your faith despite the evidence knowing that only in so doing does the evidence have any chance of changing. While I am not optimistic, I am always hopeful. ("NPR Morning Edition," April 13, 2006)

The good news that was given to the frightened and awestricken women at the empty tomb may be just the word we need today. We don't need to be afraid anymore. The Risen Christ goes before us into all of the incomplete, unfinished, confused, and often conflicted construction projects in our lives, and if our eyes are open, we will find him there.

Don't be afraid! The Risen Christ goes before us in life. He meets us in the ordinary, mundane, everyday places where we live and work, laugh and cry, suffer and rejoice, succeed and fail. And we can find him there. I have a preacher friend who likes to say that Easter means that tomorrow is never "just another day."

Don't be afraid! The Risen Christ goes before us in death, and we will find him there. Unlike Sarah Winchester, the "children of the resurrection" (Luke 20:36) don't need to hide from their own mortality. They confront the awful reality of death in the awesome assurance that Jesus has already gone before them through death, into eternal life. On Easter morning, congregations around the world celebrate that hope with Charles Wesley's words:

Soar we now where Christ has led, Alleluia!
Following our exalted Head, Alleluia!
Made like him, like him we rise, Alleluia!
Ours the cross, the grave, the skies, Alleluia!

("Christ the Lord Is Risen Today"; 1739)

William Sloane Coffin's death reminded me of one of my all-time favorite Easter sermons. He preached it at Riverside Church.

Christ's resurrection promises our own resurrection, for Christ is risen *pro nobis*, for us, to put love in our hearts, decent thoughts in our heads, and a little more iron up our spines. Christ is risen to convert us, not from life to something more than life, but from something less than life to the possibility of full life itself.

I myself believe passionately in the resurrection of Jesus Christ, because in my own life I have experienced Christ not as a memory, but as a presence. (*Living the Truth in a World of Illusions* [New York: Harper & Row, 1985], pages 70, 73)

During that same Holy Week, our congregation gathered together to celebrate the long, rich life of Bill Hopkins, a beloved physician who had birthed a major part of the population of our city. In my last visit with him, he was gravely ill, and we talked about his death and planned his memorial service. I told the congregation that the doctor had written the "prescription" for the service. Then I asked Bill the question I often ask folks in his condition: "What have you learned?" Bill's answer was as quick as it was clear. He said, "Jesus is Lord."

In his Easter sermon, William Sloane Coffin went on to tell his congregation that there is nothing sentimental about Easter. He said, "Easter represents a demand as well as a promise, a demand not that we sympathize with the crucified Christ, but that we pledge our loyalty to the risen one" (*Living the Truth in a World of Illusions*, pages 70–71).

Maybe that's what frightened those women on that first Easter morning. They had been with Jesus; they had heard what he said. Maybe it was the *demand* that scared them. Maybe that's what scares us, too. To experience the Resurrection is to discover that we, like them, are sent out to become the bearers of that good news to others. We are given the command, "Go, and tell everyone and anyone, that he is risen and he goes before you." We are called to be construction workers in the ongoing renovation of this creation into a place where the Risen Christ can take up residence.

To know the presence of the Risen Christ is to know that we are sent into the very incomplete, broken, and ragged world to bear witness to the new life that Christ came to bring. We are sent to complete the Easter story with our story, just the way other writers tried to complete the ending of Mark's Gospel by adding their own experience of the Risen Christ.

I don't know much about opera, except that it ain't over until a certain lady sings. I know enough to know that Giacomo Puccini was one of the great Italian composers, and to appreciate the story of his last work. Having gained international acclaim with *La Bohème*, *Tosca*, and *Madama Butterfly*, he began work on what would be his final creation, *Turandot*, in 1920. Before Puccini could complete the work, he was hospitalized with throat cancer. An unsubstantiated legend is that when he went into congestive heart failure, his last words were, "Remember *Turandot*."

Another composer, Franco Alfano, was given the task of completing the opera based on Puccini's outlines. The first performance was seventeen months after the death of Puccini, at La Scala, in Milan, on April 25, 1926, with Arturo Toscanini, the greatest conductor of the time, holding the baton. When they reached the point in the opera where Puccini's own work had ended, Toscanini abruptly stopped the performance, laid down his baton, turned to the stunned audience, and said, "Here the opera ends, because at this point the maestro died." He turned, walked away from the podium, the curtain came down, and the astonished audience went home with the uncompleted opera haunting their minds. But one day later the orchestra and performers returned to the stage and completed Puccini's greatest work with Alfano's ending. And that's the way it typically has been performed ever since.

Mark's dangling nonending of the Gospel offers the invitation to each of us to complete the Resurrection story with our story, to allow our lives to become the living witness to the presence of the Risen Christ. We are sent, like the frightened women at the tomb, to carry the Easter word of hope to anyone and everyone who will hear. We are invited to share in God's radical renovation of the kingdoms of this earth into the kingdom of God and of his Christ. We are engaged in an extreme makeover of our lives, our relationships, and our world into "a place where God lives through his Spirit" (Ephesians 2:22 GNT). By the power of the resurrection, we continue to pray: "Narrow is the mansion of my soul, enlarge Thou it that Thou mayest enter in."

It is a shabby way to end the Gospel. But it's a wonderful way to live!

Questions for Reflection and Discussion

1. How does the ending of Mark's Gospel strike you? Does it seem like "a shabby way to end the Gospel"? Why or why not?
2. What are some of the uncompleted projects in your life? Where are the dangling nonendings in your experience?
3. How have you, like Sarah Winchester, tried to deny the reality of death?
4. What is your personal definition of *hope*? How does the Resurrection story give hope for your life?
5. How will you complete the story of the Resurrection?

Prayer

O God, who for our redemption gave your only-begotten Son to the death of the cross, and by his glorious resurrection delivered us from the power of our enemy: Grant us so to die daily to sin, that we may evermore live with him in the joy of his resurrection; through Jesus Christ your Son our Lord, who lives and reigns with you and the Holy Spirit, one God, now and for ever. Amen. (*Book of Common Prayer,* 1979, page 222)

Focus for the Week

The Risen Christ goes before you to continue God's work of renovation in your life.